The Wild West in American History

GOLD FEVER

Written by A.I. Lake
Illustrated by Luciano Lazzarino
Edited by Arlene C. Rourke

© 1990 by Rourke Publications, Inc.

Library of Congress Cataloging-in-Publication Data

Lake, A.I., 1941-
   Gold fever / by A.I. Lake.
      p.   cm. —(The Wild West in American history)
   Summary: Describes the origins of the California Gold Rush that began in 1848, the individuals and mining techniques involved, and the resulting wealth, destruction, and tragedy.
   1. California—Gold discoveries—Juvenile literature.
2. California—Description and travel—1848-1869—Juvenile literature. 3. Gold mines and mining—California—History—19th century—Juvenile literature. [1. Gold mines and mining—California—History—19th century. 2. California—Gold discoveries.] I. Series.
F865.L23 1990
979.4′04—dc20   89-34528
                                                       CIP
   ISBN 0-86625-374-2   AC

Rourke Publications, Inc.
Vero Beach, Florida 32964

GOLD FEVER

GOLD FEVER

Since earliest times, gold has been admired for its beauty and value. Gold is strong, yet flexible; enduring, yet light. It can be stretched to a fine thread and pounded into sheets 1/300,000 of an inch. It can be shaped as easily as clay, yet it won't fall apart.

When the Spanish came to the New World in the 1550s, they were looking for El Dorado, the "Land of Gold." This was the mythical kingdom located on the Amazon River where, it was said, the streets were paved with gold.

Through the ages, men have sought gold. They have killed for it, robbed for it, and died for it. Weak nations have been exploited for it. Nations rich in gold have squandered it and collapsed when they were mined out. Gold has been responsible for the rise and fall of great nations.

THE NEW EL DORADO

John Sutter.
(Photo courtesy of California State Library.)

*J*anuary 28, 1848, was a fateful day. In his diary, John Sutter wrote this account: " 'My God, didn't I tell you to lock the door?' cried Jim Marshall. He was in a terrible state of excitement and I had all the trouble in the world to quiet him." Sutter went on to say that Marshall then showed him the small bits of yellow metal he had discovered at Sutter's mill.

Using Sutter's encyclopedia, the two men put the samples to all the tests—pounding it, weighing it, immersing it in nitric acid. There was no doubt. It was gold. Sutter's first reaction was: trouble.

Sutter was born Johann August Sutter. A German-born Swiss, he left his wife and four children in 1834 to escape debt and make a new start in America. He changed his name and settled in Missouri. In 1838 he left for California, arriving mid-year 1839. Years later the governor of Mexico, Juan Bautista Alvarado, granted Sutter 49,000 acres of land anywhere in the Sacramento Valley.

Sutter chose that land well, traveling for days up and down the American River. Noticing the rich, rolling land, he saw that a certain clearing would make an excellent fort. There, he built his fort with adobe clay, fencing it in with walls eighteen feet high and three feet thick. He prospered for a few years.

In 1841, the Russian ship *Constantine* arrived and offered to sell Sutter the Russian fur-trading posts in California—one eighty miles and the other fifty miles north of San Francisco. Sutter's empire was expanding. Soon he had blacksmith and carpentry shops, a gristmill, blanket-weaving and tannery shops, and orchards with apple, pear, peach and olive trees. He named his fort New Helvetia and, because he was situated on the overland route between the United States and California, his fort was the common stopping-off point for Americans migrating to California.

In 1847 Sutter decided to build a sawmill up the American River in the foothills of the Sierra Nevada Mountains. He made an arrangement with James Wilson Marshall, a carpenter, to build and run the mill. In return Marshall would share the lumber.

Sutter liked his domain. It ran well and made him prosperous. Now gold had been discovered. The thought of prospectors tramping across his land and scattering his herds disturbed Sutter. When he went up to the mill to look at the gold for himself, he could see that it was there in quantity. He asked the men at the mill to keep it a secret so that he could do spring planting before gold seekers appeared on his land.

In February, 1848, Sutter tried to confirm his claim to the land around the sawmill. The United States Claim Office refused, because news of the treaty ending the Mexican War had not reached California and it was not known that Mexico had legally ceded California to the United States. Sutter tried to make the best of things and began mining in the summer of 1848. He was not a miner, though, and he did better selling services to the miners. As a new town grew up—Sacramento City—with the gold rush in 1848, Sutter's boats between Sacramento and San Francisco did a booming business.

The early prospectors from the California area—in 1848—were respectful of Sutter's property. As the gold rush grew, however, the prospectors of 1849 robbed Sutter unmercifully. They stole his cattle and grain. They even stole the mill stones which they used to crush gold-bearing rock. When Sutter set up stables and shops, the men he hired cheated him.

John Sutter had the opportunity to become one of the most important men in California

James Wilson Marshall.
(Photo courtesy of California State Library.)

Sutter's Mill, El Dorado County, California.
(Photo courtesy of California State Library.)

People from all over the world came to California, drawn by the lust for gold.

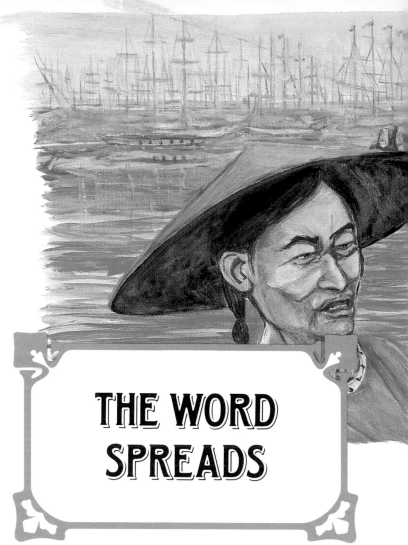

history when gold was discovered. Instead, he let it ruin him.

When Sutter was unable to claim mineral rights to his land, he was powerless to stop the miners. Once the news spread, nearly everyone from San Francisco left for the diggings—teachers, blacksmiths, doctors, tailors, and clergymen. John Sutter tried to deal with all these people flocking onto his land. He had always prided himself on being friendly and helpful to strangers. However, as his own workmen left and the gold hunters increased, he could not continue helping these strangers. "Great hosts [of people] continue to the Mountains," he wrote in his diary—it was the last thing he wrote. All the beautiful days at Sutter's Fort had come to an end.

Sutter's son came from Switzerland and found him living royally while debts mounted. The son saved his father's financial situation, but the old Sutter managed to get control of the money again. The rest of the family came to join him, but Sutter's high living created more problems. Soon he lost all his property and he and his wife fled to the East when squatters burned down their house. They settled in Pennsylvania where Sutter died at the age of 77 in 1880.

John Wilson Marshall has been called the "saddest figure of the California Gold Rush." With Sutter, he tried to claim ownership of the property on which he discovered the gold. Failing that, he tried to charge commission for any gold that prospectors found. He haggled with the miners so much that they finally rebelled and attacked the millhands and drove Marshall off the land.

With luck against him, Marshall dug himself into deeper trouble. He told people he had supernatural powers to determine where the richest deposits were. When he didn't come through with a strike, the miners threatened to lynch him. He fled for his life and tried to become a miner, but people recognized his face and greedy miners followed him everywhere.

With all this harassment, Marshall turned into a bitter man. He felt the world owed him something for his sensational discovery. He became a recluse and was forced to live off handyman jobs until his death in 1885, at the age of seventy-three.

THE WORD SPREADS

*S*utter and Marshall may have wanted to keep the gold discovery quiet, but the workers at the mill did not. One man in particular made sure everyone knew.

Sam Brannan was a store owner in Sutterville, a settlement just a few miles south of Sutter's Fort. Being a good businessman, Brannan was interested in the gold—not to dig for—but to do business with the miners. When the millhands spread the news, Brannan went up and collected a bottle of gold dust for himself. With this prize, he boarded a boat to San Francisco and ran through the streets shouting "Gold! From the American River!" In short order, Brannan had plenty of business outfitting prospectors.

Businessman Sam Brannan, however, survived the changes well. He left Sutterville and moved his store to Sacramento. In one year, Brannan made a profit of $160,000 from a hotel he ran.

News of the gold rush didn't reach the rest of the States until President James K. Polk made a formal announcement on December 5, 1848. The real migration began in 1849—hence the name "Forty-Niners."

THE FORTY-NINERS

At the beginning of 1849, the Forty-Niners were on their way! "The streets are paved with gold," newspapers along the East coast boldly stated. "It sparkles in the sands of the California Valleys," eyewitnesses were said to report. News even reached Europe, Australia, and China. With images of gold-lined streams and streets, people from other countries headed toward the American West.

The mining businesses flourished. Factories that manufactured picks, pans, shovels, boots, and mining clothing were busier than they had ever been. Gun outlets—from Boston to St. Louis—withstood business twenty-four hours a day. It is said that pawnbrokers traded more that year than in the ten previous years. Everyone seemed to want to cash in their possessions to go west—farmers left their fields, doctors their patients, carpenters their wood.

Miners, whether they were leaving by ship around Cape Horn, through the jungles of Panama, or overland on the blistering plains, sang a common song. Its tune belonged to Stephen Foster's "Oh Susanna," and the words were:

> "I soon shall be in San Francisco
> And then I'll look around,
> And when I see the gold lumps there
> I'll pick them off the ground.
>
> "Oh, Californi-o,
> That's the land for me!
> I'm going to Sacramento
> With my washbowl on my knee."

Six years after Jim Marshall discovered gold at the sawmill, the placer gold gave out. In 1848 a man could dig out about a pound of gold dust a day (then worth about $200). In 1849 and 1850 a man could find an ounce a day (about $16). After that, a miner could find only about $2.00 a day or less.

In the ten years after the discovery at Sutter's sawmill, $555 million in gold passed through San Francisco banks. On that fateful day in January 1848, no one could have guessed that Jim Marshall's one discovery of a few grains of gold would be known from China to Australia and would start a migration that would open the West.

It was the dream of quick riches that motivated the migration. It was a story that had universal appeal. The rushers, like the pioneers, were not content with what they had. Many of these people had left their original country to improve their condition and, with the gold rush, they left their second country for a "new land"—the West. They were hungry for fortune, and they were sure that it was right around the corner. Still, fortune did not always bring happiness. The desire for prosperity spurred these gold rushers on with a focused, restless passion. Even the disappointments and hardships of the journey didn't dull this glorious image of getting rich quick!

THE CAPE HORN ROUTE

Many New Englanders, being seafaring people, elected to travel around Cape Horn at the tip of South America. Any old tub that could be fit with a sail carried the advertisement declaring the going rate for the voyage to California—$300. Every inch of every scheduled ship was full. The Forty-Niners sailed over rough stormy seas through the winter. For those lucky travelers who got a good ship with a good captain, this trip around Cape Horn was the safest and most comfortable. Not many found sea-worthy vessels. Most got herded onto broken-down boats where they slept on deck, even on curled rope—anything to stay away from the furnace-like spaces below deck.

The most dangerous part of this journey occurred as the ship navigated the Cape. The winds were icy and fierce, often forcing the ships to spend weeks trying to make headway around the Cape. Some might try to cut through the Strait of Magellan, but the crosscurrents and riptides often pushed the ships off course, sometimes dangerously close to cliffs and reefs. Obviously, many ships didn't make it. Some voyagers filled their diaries with descriptions of floating wreckage. Long after the gold rush was over, families still searched for missing Forty-Niners who had sailed the high seas around the Cape.

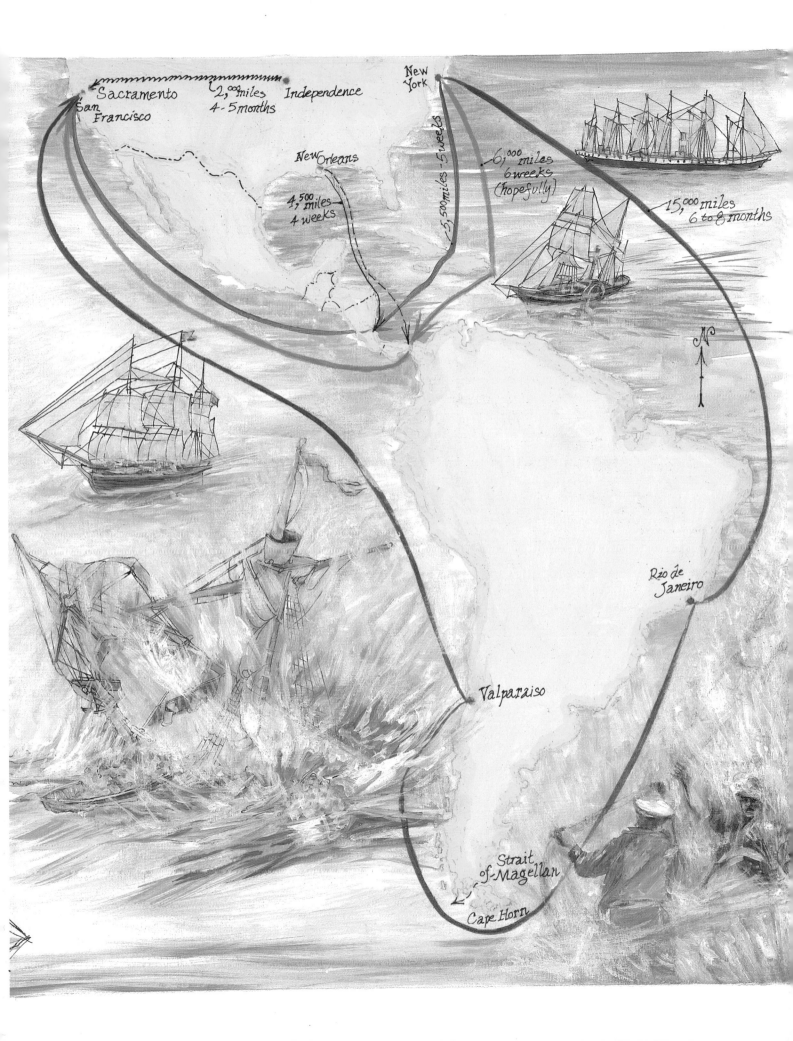

THE PANAMA SHORTCUT

Gold seekers who started out from the South and Midwest chose the shorter route through the Isthmus of Panama. If all went well, it took only four months to reach San Francisco. When the ship unloaded at the mouth of the Chagres River, which flowed through a dense jungle, the troubles began.

Natives charged high prices to take prospectors up river; sometimes they took the money and baggage and ran away. Still, no price was too high, for it was the only way the prospectors would get to their gold. Lucky prospectors finally did get on small boats that natives paddled with long poles. Monkeys, parrots, and other exotic birds chattered from trees laden with bright purple and yellow flowers. Forty-Niners said this part of the trip was unforgettable for its hot steamy days with swarming mosquitos and its nights spent in crude native villages. Many came down with cholera from the crowded, unsanitary conditions.

Some miners went by mule across Panama. At first the natives charged only twenty dollars, plus six dollars for the bags. As more gold hunters came, the natives raised their prices. Prospectors had to travel over old trails that were now worn and slippery. Heat made the travelers sick. They couldn't get off the mules to walk because they were afraid of the deadly snakes. Travel up and down the mountainsides was slow and painful.

The sight of Panama City made it all worthwhile. Spanish houses and beautifully landscaped gardens replaced the shabby huts the prospectors had seen along the Chagres River. Many were tempted to stay right in Panama. "But there's no gold here!" they were reminded, and so they set sail for San Francisco. The trip from Panama to San Francisco usually took only a month.

OVERLAND: THE HARDEST JOURNEY

*W*hile 40,000 people came by sea to California, some 100,000 more traveled over the plains and mountains to seek their fortune. Some followed the Santa Fe Trail to Santa Fe and from there they chose one of many routes to California. Or, further north, some traveled on the Oregon and Mormon Trails, over the Rocky Mountains into the Columbia River Valley toward the California Trail.

The Forty-Niners formed companies and tried to include ten to thirty wagons in a train. They chose a captain, whose orders had to be obeyed, and they abided by strict codes within their companies. The young men went on ahead to scout good trails, and each man took turns guarding the camps at night. Fearful that they might starve on the trail, prospectors overbought supplies and headed out with heavy burdens.

At first it was exciting, rolling over green grass and through meadows rich with flowers. However, the wagons were so heavy they could cover only about fifteen miles a day. Often, prospectors pitched excess food and baggage by the side of the road. Other wagon trains would pick up what they needed or could carry. Later, some prospectors deliberately hindered their fellow prospectors and destroyed any goods they threw off as excess so that no one else could reuse them.

Herds of buffalo sometimes scared the horses and mules pulling the wagons. Food ran low; prospectors had to share and ration it. The desert was parching and water was scarce. Mountain passes were narrow, so heavy ropes were tied around trees and wagons were let down by the ropes. All in all, a slow, painful journey.

THE MINING CAMPS

Word went out that anyone could find gold nuggets lying around California like hen's eggs. Everyone came for the overnight "strike"—but few found it.

Some did. One miner on the Yuba River took out thirty pounds of gold in less than a month from a claim only four square feet!

Near Angel's Camp, a man known as Raspberry accidentally struck a rock with his rifle while hunting deer. The rock broke open displaying thick veins of gold. In three days, Raspberry dug out $7,000 worth of gold.

Four men at Durgan's Flat, near Downieville, hit on $12,900 worth of gold in eleven days. In six months that sixty foot square claim produced $80,000 worth of gold.

At Carson Hill, a miner found a nugget that weighed 150 pounds. He sold it for $74,000. In the rush that followed, Carson Hill produced $2,800,000 in ten months.

Lode-gold was another rich source. Gold-bearing quartz rocks are crushed to extract the gold. One October day in 1850 George McKnight, a man from the settlement of Grass Valley, went looking for a stray cow. He stubbed his toe on some white quartz and a piece broke off. It was filled with veins of gold. The end of that vein still hasn't been found to this day! Mining companies have worked it constantly since 1850, carrying out more than $80 million in gold. One mining shaft is more than 1,600 feet below sea-level.

When someone had a good digging tale, the news traveled fast. A camp that had swelled with miners one day could be deserted the day after a new story passed through. Each time a camp was established, the miners set up new rules for the diggings. The most important rule protected individual claims. Most of the miners were young. They were full of good will and believed in fair play. If anyone broke the miners' code of ethics, he was severely punished—

Being temporary, mining camps were simple and crude. In winter, miners banded together for warmth and companionship.

hanged, branded, or banished without any trial.

On Sundays the miners rested—that is, they didn't mine. Instead, they cleaned their equipment, clothes, and held Sunday meetings to settle disputes. Women were rare—only about eight percent of the mining camp population.

At first, the camps were nearly crime-free. However, as word about the wealth got around, gamblers and thieves moved in. Some enterprising types would load a shotgun with gold dust and fire it at a rock, creating a rich lode. This was called "salting." These crooks would then try to sell claims to the phony mines. The humorist, Mark Twain, described a mine as "nothing more than a hole in the ground with a liar on top."

A simple, crude mining cabin at Cripple Creek, Colorado.

(Photo courtesy of Colorado Historical Society.)

CAMP HEALTH

*S*ome doctors have estimated that one out of five gold rushers who set out in 1849 died within six months of reaching California. Along the way, gold hunters experienced the extremes of cold and heat, starvation, scurvy, and other diseases. When they reached California, and San Francisco in particular, more problems faced them. In the city, people threw spoiled food and the intestines of slaughtered animals into the streets and yards. Gold seekers dealt with cholera, malaria, yellow fever, and dysentery.

It was no better when they got to the camps,

A photograph of the Vallejo Street wharf in San Francisco shows a settled, more comfortable way of life.
(Photo courtesy of California State Library.)

where crude shelters were put up in a day. The miners could not provide themselves with food or sanitation as they scratched the earth for the gold they had come so far to get.

There were plenty of doctors to treat miners—at least 1,500 doctors came along with the gold rush. However, there were no real professional standards, so the doctors represented the best and the worst of their profession.

Usually they approached fever as a poison to be flushed out of the system, and they'd do this by bleeding the patient. A simple jack-knife cut into a vein at the right place could do it, or often they starved leeches and applied them to skin that had been spread with cream or sugar. Sometimes doctors did not watch how much blood they were taking, and many patients bled to death.

These were the conditions of the gold rush. In some ways, it is amazing that only one-fifth of the gold seekers died. Historians have observed that California was a warm, pleasant land where people could sustain themselves easily. In fact, one said that few other places in the world could have sustained "a gathering of humanity so well."

One of the things going for the gold prospectors was their vivacious, hearty spirit. They kept vigorous and resilient; they were men who could handle anything. The qualities that got them into trouble were the same that got them out.

One gold rusher wrote about San Francisco, "Of all the cities in the world, this is the greatest one, composed of all nations and colors, and the hairiest set of fellows that ever existed."

THE DONNER PARTY

The hardships were terrible. Some stories ended tragically. The Donner party was trapped in the Sierra Nevadas during the winter of 1846-7. They had miscalculated the time it would take them to cross the pass before winter storms set in. When many of their party died, the only way the rest could survive was by cannibalism.

When the Forty-Niners finally ran out of food, most didn't resort to cannibalism, but some did have to eat their oxen. When they finally came through the low desert valley, some were heard to say, "Good-bye, Death Valley!" The name has stuck to this day.

For many, it took a whole year to reach the gold fields of California. When they finally arrived at the diggings, they were a tired, hungry, worn out lot. Many died on the way. Those that had survived, however, were more ready than their seafaring brothers to withstand the rigors of mining.

An old prospector panning for gold.

MINING FOR GOLD

For real miners, digging for gold was hard work. A miner set out with just a pan, squatting by the stream's edge and scooping up about half a panful of dirt and plenty of water. He'd swish the contents around, tipping the pan so that the sand spilled out. With a few deft twists, all the sand was gone and only a few flakes of gold remained. Gold is about eight times heavier than sand so it sinks to the bottom while the lighter sand rises to the surface and spills over the edge. A miner needed to learn exactly how to swirl a pan so that precious gold specks would not be lost. Panning was impractical, however, and very time consuming.

Miners soon began to use cradles or rockers, which looked much like a baby's cradle. The top was covered with an iron plate punctured with many holes. The base was slanted and lined with ridges. The miner shoveled dirt on the plate and then rocked the cradle back and forth, pouring water over the dirt. Stones rolled off, sand and gold settled to the bottom where they were caught by the ridges. The lighter sand washed away.

Operating a cradle was difficult. One miner said is was like the old trick of patting the top of your head with one hand while rubbing your stomach with the other. It required two people

Sluicing for gold called for a cooperative effort by many miners. (Photo courtesy of California State Library.)

though three was perfect; one man dug, one carried dirt to the rocker, and the third worked the rocker itself. The cradle took mining from an individual enterprise to a business.

In time, the cradle was deemed too slow. It gave way to the long tom, which worked like a cradle but was larger. It was placed right in the stream so that the water ran through it. After the gold was panned, each man was given his share.

As rich sands grew scarce, miners were forced to give up their independence. They went to the next tool, the sluice box, which was expensive to build and definitely could not be managed alone. The sluice was a long line of open boxes joined together; they had rifle bars on the bottom to catch the gold. Some miners made them fifty to one hundred feet long. They placed one end of the sluice where the stream could run through it, and miners shoveled gravel into the sluice boxes. All who worked the box shared what they found. If no gold was found, they had to move on again.

Coyoting was another method miners tried. Here they sunk a shaft straight down through the earth to reach the bedrock—sometimes 150 feet below the surface. If there was gold, it was usually at the bottom. This kind of mining was dangerous, for the mines sometimes caved in.

Hydraulic mining used water that was brought in long ditches or wooden troughs called flumes. Water was sent through hoses and sprayed against the rocks, causing the rocks to crumble and fall into sluice boxes below.

Through a long-barreled cannon, the hoses "fired" water at the rocks, blasting away everything in its path. Hydraulic mining was not good for the environment. Mountains gave way, forests were undermined, and all the refuse was dumped into the rivers. When miners had to stop hydraulic mining, they adopted another destructive method—dredging. They used huge floating

The long tom was worked by several men. (Photo courtesy of California State Library.)

Fire was a constant danger. This rare 1896 photograph shows part of the town of Cripple Creek, Colorado, in flames. (Photo courtesy of Colorado Historical Society.)

dredges wherever the gold-veined earth was fairly level. The dredge began where it could float and then sucked in topsoil as it moved across land. Sluices separated the rock and gravel and piled up silt, which in turn ruined acres of good farmland.

In 1884 the state legislature put a stop to hydraulic mining in California, but it was too late for many areas. Today, the destruction is still seen in the foothills of the Sierra Nevada Mountains—a sad display of human greed.

Hydraulic mining and dredging could only have been financed by big business, so after the prohibition of hydraulic mining, business introduced a new cyanide process. Gold mining, for all practical purposes, left the arena of the individual and remained in the hands of big business.

The lone prospector, with his washbowl on his knee, became an old symbol of a spirited age, full of enthusiasm and goodwill. Such an age hasn't been seen again.

Mining operations underway in Cripple Creek. (Photo courtesy of Colorado Historical Society.)

BRINGING GLAMOUR TO THE WEST

*A*ctresses came to the camps with touring companies, and they were so welcome they were treated like royalty. Mostly, miners entertained themselves. At night, the men would play music and half of them would tie bandanas around their arms and pretend to be the "ladies" for dancing with the "gents."

No story of the Gold Rush would be complete without mentioning two women who brought glamour to the Northern Mines.

Lola Montez was born in Ireland and created a sensation all over Europe when she performed on stage. In 1852, she made a tour of America, packing in audiences from New York to San Francisco. Her beauty and notoriety intrigued people.

Lola finally decided to retire and moved into a house that is still standing in San Francisco. Many children walked by her house on their way to school. One day seven-year-old Lotta Crabtree stopped for a visit. The two became friends and Lola taught Lotta some songs and dances. The child learned easily and began performing for Lola's guests.

About a year later, the Crabtrees moved away, separating Lola and Lotta. By that time Lotta was ready to go out on her own. At the age of eight, she went on stage and the miners showered her with gold coins and nuggets. Lotta's successful career was launched. She toured the mines for years, and eventually went to San Francisco and then on the New York and international fame.

Her teacher, Lola Montez, was not so lucky. She tried to tour again—this time in Australia—but failed there also. Lola returned to the United States and began lecturing, but she failed at that as well. She became ill and died at 43 in 1861. In that same year, Lotta was just achieving fame in San Francisco. Lola did succeed at one thing, however. She saw and encouraged the talent of the young Lotta, and took her under her wing.

THE POLITE POET-ROBBER

With gold came thieves. All that precious metal being transported all over the country was sure to attract highway robbers—and it did! One of the more unusual outlaws was Black Bart.

This stagecoach robber was the "Dr. Jekyll and Mr. Hyde" of the West. At times, he was a mild-mannered shipping clerk—Charles Bolton—who worked in stagecoach offices. At other times, "Black Bart" scared the living daylights out of stagecoach drivers when he would quietly step from the brush with his shotgun. Very politely, he'd call out, "Will you please throw down your treasure box, sir?"

Bart was always gentle with his victims, never hurting the driver or passengers. Later, people learned that he never owned a single shell for his shotgun. Even in self-defense, he couldn't have fired it.

His outfits were just as strange. He wore a long linen duster with a flour sack over his head. Of course he cut holes for the eyes, and he always traveled on foot. He carried a blanket roll with an axe tucked into it. He used the axe to open the treasure boxes.

Black Bart had studied the routes of the coaches and chose his attacks carefully. They were always at sharp bends where the horses would be moving slowly.

Still, he was even more eccentric: he was a poet. He left bits of poems at the scene of some of his early robberies. The poems haven't survived, but the signature he put on them has. He signed them "Black Bart, the PO8" (po-eight).

When he was finally caught, the whole story came out. He was wounded while escaping from a robbery near Copperopolis. He accidentally dropped a handkerchief that the laundry had marked "FX07." The police traced the mark and made what was considered one of the most surprising arrests in San Francisco's history.

Black Bart turned out to be Charles E. Bolton, one of the city's leading citizens, as well as a person with many contacts at the police department.

The mild-mannered Charles Bolton was born Charles E. Boles, and he grew up in Illinois where he received an excellent education. After serving in the Civil War, he moved to California in search of gold. When that search didn't pan out, he took up highwaymanship.

In August, 1877, he changed into Black Bart and performed his first holdup on the Point Arena-Duncan Mill's stage, near the Russian River. Because he had studied the schedules, he found the job easy. So he kept doing it.

With success came riches. Bart moved to San Francisco and changed his name to Charles Bolton. People saw him as a prominent member of the highest social circles. So whenever he needed more cash to support his extravagant lifestyle, he put away his respectable derby and donned his flour sack.

He was sentenced to six years at San Quentin, but was released early for good behavior. No one knows what eventually happened to the dignified Charles E. Boles, the most famous stage robber of the West.

The California Gold Rush will always be remembered for its economic and historic importance, but also for its raft of unique characters.

The miners were fiercely loyal to the rules of the camp—especially since they were the ones who made up the rules. Gradually, the rules spread throughout all the camps and became known as the Miners' Ten Commandments. In 1853, they were enacted into Federal Law. They were lengthy and written with flourish. Here is a shortened version.

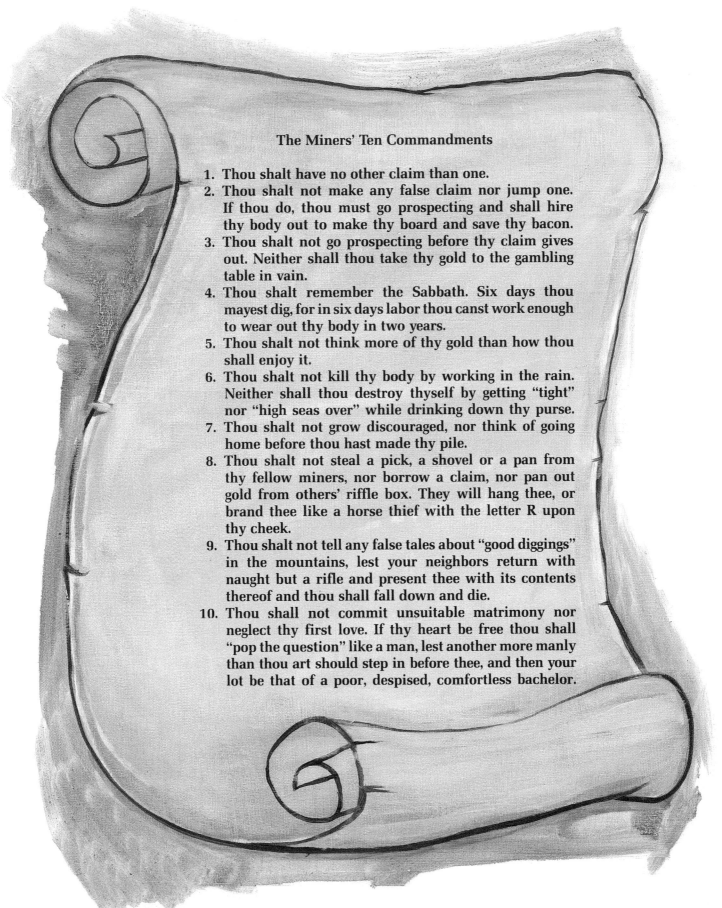

The Miners' Ten Commandments

1. Thou shalt have no other claim than one.
2. Thou shalt not make any false claim nor jump one. If thou do, thou must go prospecting and shall hire thy body out to make thy board and save thy bacon.
3. Thou shalt not go prospecting before thy claim gives out. Neither shall thou take thy gold to the gambling table in vain.
4. Thou shalt remember the Sabbath. Six days thou mayest dig, for in six days labor thou canst work enough to wear out thy body in two years.
5. Thou shalt not think more of thy gold than how thou shall enjoy it.
6. Thou shalt not kill thy body by working in the rain. Neither shall thou destroy thyself by getting "tight" nor "high seas over" while drinking down thy purse.
7. Thou shalt not grow discouraged, nor think of going home before thou hast made thy pile.
8. Thou shalt not steal a pick, a shovel or a pan from thy fellow miners, nor borrow a claim, nor pan out gold from others' riffle box. They will hang thee, or brand thee like a horse thief with the letter R upon thy cheek.
9. Thou shalt not tell any false tales about "good diggings" in the mountains, lest your neighbors return with naught but a rifle and present thee with its contents thereof and thou shall fall down and die.
10. Thou shall not commit unsuitable matrimony nor neglect thy first love. If thy heart be free thou shall "pop the question" like a man, lest another more manly than thou art should step in before thee, and then your lot be that of a poor, despised, comfortless bachelor.

Emigrants crossing the plains.
(Photo courtesy of Oregon Historical Society.)

THE END OF AN ERA

At the peak of the Gold Rush, over 120,000 miners were digging for gold in California. By 1873, there were only 30,000, half of whom were Chinese. Where did they go, and what did they think about their adventure?

Many miners went back home, disillusioned when they found that their dreams were nothing like real life. Some went home because of persecution—the French, Chinese, and Latin Americans were among these. Many Yankees ran "furriners" out of the best mining locations. The Foreign Miners Tax was the cruelest act of all: it stated that all miners who were not citizens had to pay $20 a month to be able to mine, and the fee had to be renewed monthly.

Some miners were just the roaming type. They followed fortune wherever it called. They lived on rumors and flimsy promises.

Most stayed right in California—even after they realized that they would never strike it rich. They mined with the companies for another thirty years. They worked in mills, foundries, or shops. After 1860, California became better known for its agriculture than its mining.

Not many hopefuls got rich from the Gold Rush, but many found a new life in California. By 1869, the first transcontinental railroad was completed, opening up the entire West as we know it.

Historians say that the importance of the Gold Rush didn't lay in the millions of dollars in gold it produced, but in the fact that it happened when it did, at a time when America had just extended its borders to the Pacific Ocean. In a way, these California gold hunters achieved more importance as settlers than as miners.

The gold rush is the story of every immigrant's dream of freedom and wealth. It is the symbol of a country's discovery and mastery of its natural resources.

GETTING THE GOLD OUT

*L*uck and hard work. Bringing gold out of the California foothills during the Gold Rush depended on luck and hard, dangerous work.

Within those few decades that we call the Gold Rush, mining gold went from a simple one-man technique to a huge business.

Panning

Gold panning was a technique that was many centuries old when the Forty-Niners began using it. It was pretty simple: the miner shoveled some gravel into a shallow pan and swirled it around. The lighter sand spilled over the side, while the heavier stuff—like gold—settled in the bottom of the pan.

The problem with panning was it was too slow. It took about 20 minutes to pick gold particles from a single pan. On a good day, a miner could wash out about 50 pans.

Rocking the Cradle

Like panning, the rocker (or cradle) was a simple technique, too. A rectangular box was mounted on rockers. The miners shoveled gravel on to the top sieve and poured a bucket of water over it. Then they rocked the mixture to send it flowing into the box, where the cleats at the bottom of the box caught the heavy gold.

It was quicker than panning, but the miners had to be near water to make the rocker work. Still, two men working a rocker could wash a cubic yard a day.

The Long Tom

Improving on the cradle, the miners just enlarged the box so that it had a ten- to twenty-foot trough. They fitted the trough with a sheet of perforated metal which covered the riffle box. Two men shoveled the dirt into the top of the long tom, and a third would throw out big rocks. Only once or twice a day did they have to stop and remove the gold.

Sluicing

Sluice boxes were just longer versions of the long tom. The men put several sluice boxes together to keep a whole crew of miners busy shoveling gravel into the troughs.

Sometimes they made sluices right in the ground—like shallow ditches. Then they would send the loose gravel down the ditch to a sluice box at the bottom where they'd pan out the gold.

Hydraulic Mining

Hydraulic mining was the most efficient and most destructive way to get the gold out. It was based simply on water pressure directed against soft banks. The force of the water caved in the banks and the dirt washed downhill into a series of sluice boxes that would separate the gold from the other materials. In the end, the system proved not to be very efficient. Too much gold got away with the fast moving water and gravel.

IN THE DAYS OF THE GOLD RUSH

1839	John Sutter arrives in Sacramento Valley to start first inland settlement in northern California.
1846	War begins between U.S. and Mexico.
1846	A heavy winter traps the Donner immigrant wagon train in the Sierra, killing 39 of 87 members.
January 24, 1848	James Marshall picks up small piece of metal while examining tailrace at partially completed sawmill.
1848	The treaty is signed ending the Mexican War and the California Territory is ceded to the U.S.
March, 1848	The first story of gold discovery is printed in a San Francisco newspaper.
December, 1848	President Polk's message to Congress confirms the California gold discovery.
February, 1849	*California*, the first steamship, arrives in San Francisco with a load of Forty-Niners.
May, 1849	The first train of overland prospectors begins in Missouri.
July, 1849	The first of the overland wagons arrives in the Sacramento Valley.
October, 1849	The first of the European emigrants arrives.
Winter, 1849	Some 42,000 hopefuls arrive by land and another 39,000 by sea.
1850	Yankee dislike for foreigners results in Foreign Miners Tax of $20 a month.
1850	California is admitted into the Union as the thirty-first state.
1853	E.E. Matteson invents hydraulic mining.
April 13, 1860	The first west-bound rider of the Pony Express arrives in San Francisco.
1861	Mark Twain arrives in the West.
1880	John Sutter dies in Pennsylvania.
1884	The Sawyer Decision closes all hydraulic mines in California.
1885	James Wilson Marshall, the man whose discovery started the gold rush, dies at the age of seventy-three.